THE BATTLE PLAN

THE BATTLE PLAN

EXPERIENCING JOY THROUGH THE TRIAL

JANEÉ WILLIAMS

Trilogy Christian Publishers

A Wholly Owned Subsidiary of Trinity Broadcasting Network

2442 Michelle Drive

Tustin, CA 92780

Copyright © 2025 by Janeé Williams

All Scripture quotations, unless otherwise noted, are taken from the New King James Version®. Copyright © 1982 by Thomas Nelson. Used by permission. All rights reserved.

Scripture quotations marked niv are taken from the Holy Bible, New International Version®, NIV®. Copyright © 1973, 1978, 1984, 2011 by Biblica, Inc.TM Used by permission of Zondervan. All rights reserved worldwide. www.zondervan.com. The "NIV" and "New International Version" are trademarks registered in the United States Patent and Trademark Office by Biblica, Inc.TM

Scripture quotations marked nlt are taken from the Holy Bible, New Living Translation, copyright © 1996, 2004, 2015 by Tyndale House Foundation. Used by permission of Tyndale House Publishers, Inc., Carol Stream, Illinois 60188. All rights reserved.

Scripture quotations marked (KJV) are taken from The Holy Bible, King James Version. Cambridge Edition: 1769.

All rights reserved, including the right to reproduce this book or portions thereof in any form whatsoever.

For information, address Trilogy Christian Publishing

Rights Department, 2442 Michelle Drive, Tustin, CA 92780.

Trilogy Christian Publishing/ TBN and colophon are trademarks of Trinity Broadcasting Network.

For information about special discounts for bulk purchases, please contact Trilogy Christian Publishing.

Trilogy Disclaimer: The views and content expressed in this book are those of the author and may not necessarily reflect the views and doctrine of Trilogy Christian Publishing or the Trinity Broadcasting Network.

10 9 8 7 6 5 4 3 2 1

Library of Congress Cataloging-in-Publication Data is available.

ISBN 979-8-89597-056-0

ISBN 979-8-89597-057-7

DEDICATION

I dedicate this book first to my Lord and Savior, Jesus Christ. I can do all things through Him who strengthens me and I am nothing without Him. Thank You, Lord, for using me and allowing me to share what You have done for me in this season. I love You, Abba!

To my mother, Crystal Williams, who turned to me on the day of my diagnosis and expressed that we had to fight! Those words ignited something in me and encouraged me to begin the battle plan in my life. Thank you, Mommy, I love you!

To my father, Ronald Williams, thank you for your deep support and love as I stepped through this trial. Your humor, encouraging words, faith, and strength helped me in more ways than you know! I love you, Daddy!

To my siblings, Dashawn, Ron, and Kristen, thank you for your unwavering support. You listened, you encouraged, you showed up, and you loved me every step of the way. I love you!

To Sydni, Jarikka, Nora, and Odessa, thank you! Your constant prayers, love, support, and strength were refreshing as I walked through this each day. Thank you for allowing God to use you to bless me and hold me up. I adore each of you. Thank you for being my best friends and sisters for life!

To Pastor Charles Bennett, Jr., First Lady Michelle Bennett, and the New Beginnings Christian Church family, thank you! Your faith, strength, and love helped carry me through. Thank you for always showing up. Thank you for praying with me and for me. Thank you for reminding me constantly of what God says about me and encouraging me to continue to stand on His Word. I appreciate each of you and love you dearly!

Finally, and certainly not least, to all of my family and friends who called, stopped by, encouraged, supported, prayed, and loved me along the way, thank you! I love you all, and God bless you.

"My son, attend to my words; Incline thine ear unto my sayings. Let them not depart from thine eyes; Keep them in the midst of thine heart. For they are life unto those that find them, and health to all their flesh."

(Prov. 4:20–22, KJV)

TABLE OF CONTENTS

INTRO: 9

YOUR BATTLE PLAN: 15

CHAPTER 1: HEALING IS OF TODAY
AND FOR YOU 17

CHAPTER 2: UNDERSTANDING THAT YOU
WERE/ARE HEALED 21

CHAPTER 3: GOD'S WORD HEALS 27

CHAPTER 4: RESIST THE ENEMY 31

CHAPTER 5: YOUR BODY DOESN'T DICTATE
YOUR HEALING 35

CHAPTER 6: PRAY FERVENTLY 39

CHAPTER 7: REJOICE, IT'S A TRIAL! 43

CHAPTER 8: SHARE YOUR TESTIMONY,
DON'T WAIT! 47

CHAPTER 9: YOU HAVE AUTHORITY 51

CHAPTER 10: LISTEN, SPEAK, BELIEVE 55

CHAPTER 11: CONCERN LIST 59

CHAPTER 12: COMMUNITY IS EVERYTHING 63

CHAPTER 13: GOD FINISHES WHAT HE STARTS . . 65

CHAPTER 14: MY FULL TESTIMONY 67

CHAPTER 15: HEALING SCRIPTURES............71
ENDNOTES: 87
ABOUT THE AUTHOR:........................89

INTRO

At the end of May 2023, I received the call that the mass they found in my right breast was cancerous. To say I was devastated is an understatement. I just could not believe it. This type of news is something you hear happening in the movies, or you hear from family or friends that someone they know is dealing with a cancer diagnosis, but you never think you, yourself, would be dealing with it first-hand. My mind went from zero to a million and I jumped to the worst-case scenario. My thought was, "How could I die? There has to be a mistake somewhere." I kept thinking the doctor would call me back within a few moments and tell me the scans were wrong and I was in the clear. As I waited for the call that this was all a mistake, news that would never come, I was filled with fear and anxiety.

A month, actually a matter of weeks before, my uncle passed away from leukemia, cancer of the blood. My father and mother were so wrapped up in the treatment of my uncle, traveling to see him almost every weekend and checking in via phone calls and FaceTime. This was yet another thing they'd have to carry. I felt so bad. All I could think about was each one of my family members who received a cancer diagnosis and how each of them died from it.

How could this be the plan for me? I still had so much to do! I want to get married, have a family, and walk in the full calling and purpose that God has for me. Why this? Why now? I believed in God and felt I did everything "right." How could sickness attack me? The disbelief and worry were unbearable and so heavy to carry.

I remember, after seeing the breast surgeon, sitting at home trying to explain the diagnosis to my family. At that moment, my mom turned to me, my face full of worry and unbelief, and she said, "We've got to fight." I thought, "Fight for what? What more do I have to do other than pray for healing and hope I get it?" I didn't know what she meant or what was in store for me if I allowed God into my situation and obeyed what He was about to show me. There was a joyous, yes, joyous, ride before me. God was about to draw me so near to Him, and His scripture would suddenly become so alive to me. I was in for a joyous ride indeed.

Over the next few days, as I coped with the diagnosis given by my doctors and began to share it with a few people, God started to reveal His plan for me. Can I just say that God's plans for us are so good and prosperous!

> "For I know the plans I have for you," declares the Lord, "plans to prosper you and not to harm you, plans to give you hope and a future. Then you will call on me and come and pray to me, and I will listen to you. You will seek me and find me when you seek me with all your heart."
> Jeremiah 29:11–13 (NIV)

He wants the best for us, and if we call on Him, He will listen and move on our behalf. He is such a loving God! Through my family and friends, the Lord beautifully guided me toward scriptures, testimonies, and teachings on healing. I knew about healing, but my understanding of it was starting to change. These next few chapters unfold the revelations I received as I stood on the battle plan and stepped through this beautiful journey. Proverbs 43:20–22 was not just a scripture I read through but the plan I needed to follow to step through this trial. It's not just about knowing God's scripture but meditating on it and standing on it without a doubt. Each day, I had to be intentional, choosing to give this diagnosis over to God and staying in a posture of expectation and praise.

I had to show God that I trusted Him and believed His Word, and I was excited to watch Him move on my behalf. These chapters lay out how I renewed my mind through constant connection with the Father, stood on His unwavering and powerful scripture, and clung to Jesus through it all.

THE BATTLE PLAN:

So here's the plan. I want to break it down for you here and then step you through some of the nuggets our Father shared with me as I walked this thing out. Simply put, the Battle Plan is Proverbs 4:20–22 (KJV). It's a call to action, and I believe this is the very basis for getting through any trial because it directs you to be rooted in God's Word.

"My son, attend to my words" (Prov. 4:20).

To attend is defined as paying attention to something.1 Our Father is calling us to pay attention to His Word. As followers of Christ, it is imperative that we not only follow God's Word but give attention to it. How can we truly follow God's Word if we don't study it? It is so easy to get caught up in the whirlwinds of what is popular or "hot" in the world today, but we are called to give attention to truth: God's Word. That should be our influence. What does this look like? Spending time in scripture and becoming familiar with it. To be familiar with it means to know what the Word says about you, what is promised to you, and what the Word says about our Father. There is power in knowing, without a doubt, what the Word of God says about you and confidently walking in that knowing.

"Incline thine ear unto my sayings" (Prov. 4:20).

To incline has several meanings, but the one I love is to feel favorable toward something or someone.2 This means that you favor what God has to say to you above all else. Although you may receive advice from others, you are favorable to the words of our Father. You must also favor what God has to say above what you have to say. That's a big one! Many of us solely follow our opinions. We'll consult the Father and a few others, but at the end of the day, we choose what makes us happy, not necessarily what God willed for us. If something is favored, it has an advantage over everything else. That should always be the case with the Word of God. No matter how uncomfortable it makes us, regardless of if it goes against what we choose for ourselves. It is truth, and that truth should set the precedent for how we tackle life's situations. When we give God's Word the advantage over all the opinions coming our way, including ours, we then have the advantage in the situations we face because God's Word is the foundation.

"Let them not depart from thine eyes" (Prov. 4:21).

Gosh, I love this one! The Word calls us to keep our eyes on scripture and not depart from it. Now, it's impossible to look at the Word all day, constantly. Well, you could do it, but you wouldn't get anything done. So, we must meditate on the Word throughout the day. When we can, we should be reading the Word, understanding it for ourselves, and thinking about the scriptures as much as we're able. Instead of getting on TikTok or Instagram during breaks or down time, open up the Word and read some scripture. I guarantee you'll feel better about the rest of your day if you spend some time in God's Word. What works for me is to write scripture down and place it on my computer desk or in a note on my phone so that I can view it whenever I want. We should be so full of God's Word that we don't have room for anything else.

"Keep them in the midst of thine heart" (Prov. 4:21).

To keep them in the midst of your heart means to know without a doubt that God's Word is true. The crazy thing about our bodies is that our minds will wander. That's just a fact. We see different things on social media and hear different things when we connect with other people, and that causes our mind to wander, sometimes, into some negative thoughts about what we're going through. However, even though our thoughts can get pretty negative, if we know in our hearts that we are healed, then it doesn't matter what our minds or the enemy try to convince us of. We can always go back to the heart of the matter: we are healed. So, convince yourself, in your heart, that God's Word is true. Then, when your mind wanders, because it will, silence those thoughts with what the Word says. Rebuke those thoughts. Say, "Nope, because God's Word says that I am already healed. I believe that in my heart, no matter what I see, what others say, or even what I think, I am healed in Jesus' name." You have to keep that in rotation to keep you on track and focused on the Word of God.

"For they are life unto those that find them, and health to all their flesh" (Prov. 4:22).

This is the reward! If we do the things above, we have life and health! Enough said!

YOUR BATTLE PLAN

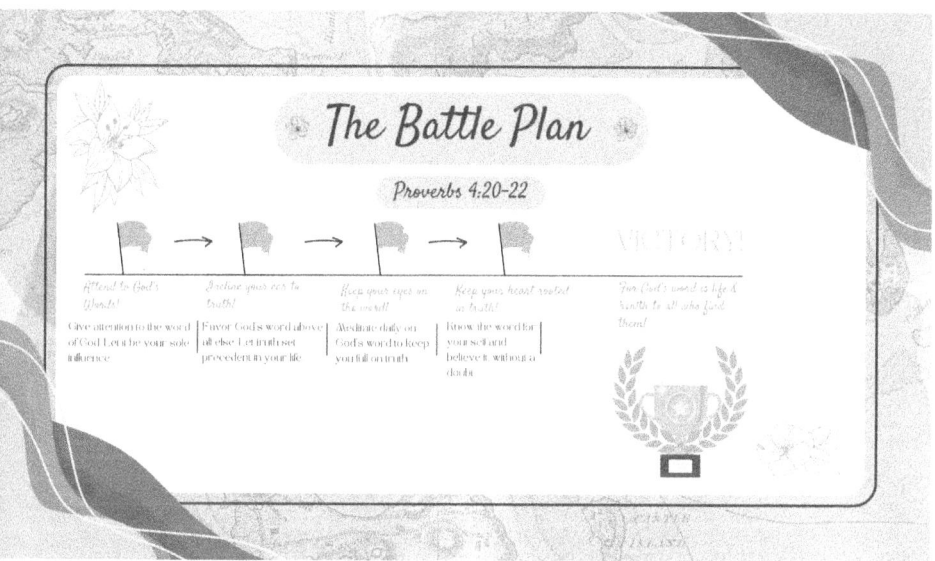

Over these next chapters, you'll see how the battle plan was activated in my life. I talk about the scriptures that not only guided me through my healing journey, but strengthened me day by day to go forward. My foundation was God's Word and God's Word alone. I constantly had to combat my flesh, the enemy, and this world trying to instill lies that didn't line up with truth. I was intentional about filling up on God's Word and believing nothing else. Here's what our Creator revealed to me as I walked through this beautiful journey.

CHAPTER 1

HEALING IS OF TODAY AND FOR YOU

"Jesus Christ is the same yesterday, and today, and forever" (Heb. 13:8).

One of the things that I had to make sure I wrapped my head around was that healing is for me. When you get diagnosed with anything, immediately you're thinking through how you can get to the other side of it. If it's a "big" diagnosis like I received, or a scary diagnosis, sometimes we think that healing can't come because we can't see it in our minds. However, the Word calls us to not lean on our own understanding:

"Trust in the Lord with all your heart, and lean not on your own understanding" (Prov. 3:5).

When I was told my diagnosis, I really couldn't see the end of the tunnel. I immediately thought that my life was over. That's a scary thing to share with you all, even as I type these words, but that's where my mind went. I jumped right to the worst-case scenario. I went to that place because I hadn't put my trust in Jesus yet to guide me through what I was about to face. It wasn't my job to understand how to get to the end of this journey. My job was simply to trust Jesus. He's got the rest. With the recent loss of my uncle to cancer weeks before, and another uncle to the same disease years before, my experience with cancer in my family was discouraging. Here's the zinger: I knew that God still healed, but was He going to heal me? Would I meet the criteria to receive healing? All this was going through my mind, yet I still hadn't given it over to the Lord. I allowed my mind to be buried in "what ifs," discouraging memories, and overwhelming fears. I was drowning in it, and I couldn't hear God even though I desperately needed Him.

Here's the beautiful thing about the unchanging hand of Jesus: it's unchanging. Although my experience with this diagnosis was more negative than positive it didn't matter because the God I serve is unchanging. He is a healer! Just like he healed the woman with the issue of blood, the man with leprosy, and even Sarah's womb, He has also healed me. He is the same yesterday, today, and forever (Heb. 13:8). Facts! What I realized is that although healing is a promise to all of us, unfortunately, not everyone experiences healing here on this earth and that could be for a lot of different reasons. One thing that I knew, I needed to make up my mind that I was healed, then I could walk in the fullness of that promise. I became determined to see God's healing manifest in my body. If God's Word says that He never changes then that means that healing is for me. No matter how deeply I buried myself in worry, fear, or unanswered questions. If I got a hold of that promise of healing, then God could pull me out of that crazy thinking and show me just what He meant and boy did He. God's Word says:

"My covenant I will not break, nor alter the word that has gone out of My lips" (Ps. 89:34).

I love this scripture because it reminds me that God isn't fickle like people can be sometimes. He doesn't say, healing is for you and then comes back later and changes His mind. God's Word says what it says. It is not only unchanging but more powerful than a two-edged sword:

"For the word of God is living and powerful, and sharper

than any two-edged sword, piercing even to the division of soul and spirit, and of joints and marrow, and is a discerner of the thoughts and intents of the heart" (Heb. 4:12).

It can cut through bone and marrow. What does that mean? There is no problem too big for our Lord:

- This situation is scary. So what?
- I can't see the other side of it. So what?
- So many of my family members passed away from the same disease. So what?
- The world has magnified this issue and instilled worry. So what?

God's Word is more powerful than that. It can cut through the mightiest of situations. We just have to believe that it will. We can get so wrapped up in the craziness of what we're going through that our problem is magnified and our God is minimized. Know this: there is nothing too big for our God. If we believe His Word, we can have confidence and peace in knowing that He has us. Just like He healed, delivered, and fixed the situations of the people in the Bible, He'll do it for us because we are His children too. When we gave our life to Him, we became His. These are simply His promises for us, His children, and He has so much in store for His children.

CHAPTER 2

UNDERSTANDING THAT YOU WERE/ARE HEALED

Gosh! This took some time before I came into the revelation of these scriptures:

> Who Himself bore our sins in His own body on the tree, that we, having died to sins, might live for righteousness—by whose stripes you were healed.
> 1 Peter 2:24
>
> But He was wounded for our transgressions, He was bruised for our iniquities; the chastisement for our peace was upon Him, and by His stripes we are healed.
> Isaiah 53:5

Now, I've heard the scripture in Isaiah my entire Christian journey: by Your stripes, we are healed. However, I can honestly say that I didn't truly get the depth of that declaration until I went through my healing journey. Man, once I got it? It was so powerful! Have you ever heard preachers say, "Man, what you just said was so good to me!"? Once I got the revelation of that word, it was so good to me!

Let me take you back before I plunge you forward. To me, healing was always something that we needed to get. I would hear of people getting sick, whether my family members or close friends, and I would hope that God would heal them. I would pray that God would heal them. Even if I was asked to pray for someone who needed healing, all I could pray over them was the scripture "by His stripes they are healed." That's all I knew, and I would command healing over their body because that's what I heard others do, but I didn't completely understand it. So my mindset was, if you say you're sick, pray for healing and hope that God will heal you.

Now, let me plunge you forward. God began to unpack the revelation of that scripture for me. First of all, He showed me that there are two places in the Bible where we see the scripture. The first is Isaiah 53:5. This one is in the present tense, "are healed." The next place is 1 Peter 2:24. This one was new to me and is in the past tense, "were healed." What He showed me is that these two scriptures do not speak of something that is on its way. It is proclaiming something that is already done. It is here. By His stripes, we were healed, and so we are healed. What does this mean? Healing is not something we need to get. When Jesus died on that Cross for our sins, that is when we received our healing. That very moment, when He took on our iniquities and infirmities on that tree and died for them, we received our healing. So God began to change my mindset on this. He showed me that I'm walking around in a healed body because of what Jesus did on the Cross for me many years ago. A healed body that is being attacked by sickness. How powerful is that! When He died on the Cross for me, my body was healed, and now the enemy is trying to attack my healed body with sickness. What a revelation.

So what did I do with this information? Every chance I got, I proclaimed I was healed. I was constantly praying over myself, speaking God's scripture over me, and proclaiming healing. At every doctor's appointment I came from, I never spoke what they said. I never once said, "I have cancer." (That feels so weird to type here, even now.) I would not allow that to be my confession. Only God's Word. What God showed me is this: how can I confess God's Word over my body, pray it over myself, allow other people to pray it over me, and then turn around and say that I have a sickness? That completely curses the blessing and the promise that I just spoke. It completely cancels out the Word of God that I just proclaimed over myself.

Too many people are walking around sick because of their confessions. They pray for healing, ask for prayer, and declare healing over themselves, and then walk away and say they have the very sickness they just rebuked. We're human and sometimes our confession is wrong; I get that. However, once we know better, we do better. Our proclamations have to change and line up with the Word of God. With that in mind, I made sure I always said, "They say I have this thing, but God says that I'm healed, and that's all that matters." That continued to be my confession throughout this journey. I wouldn't accept anything else.

I'll tell you a bit of a funny story. At my church, I work the altar on Sunday mornings. We have a small, quaint church, so when we do altar calls some Sundays, there aren't a lot of people, and this was the case this Sunday. There were about two people up there, one of them being one of my best friends. As we're waiting for more people to come up, she turns to me and says, "I should be behind you so you can get some prayer for healing." I immediately said, with the neck roll and all, "No, I'm healed. I'm good." She kind of looked at me like, "Sorry, I was trying to help." The Lord immediately convicted me at that moment. I went back and apologized and explained to her what I meant. There was so much behind my reaction, but I didn't have the words or the time, quite frankly, to get it all out since we were about to start the altar call.

What I meant was that I was in a really good headspace about my situation. I knew that I was healed already, and I didn't need to take up space on the altar for more prayer for myself when someone else could come up and get the prayer they needed. Mind you, although my intentions were good, the thought I had was not a good one. The altar is for anyone, and you can come up as many times as you want to get what you need. Even if the word is the same each time. You do what you need to do. The Word says:

"Keep on asking, and you will receive what you ask for. Keep on seeking, and you will find. Keep on knocking, and the door will be opened to you" (Matt. 7:7, NLT).

This was the mindset my best friend had. She wanted me to continue to seek God in prayer until we saw the complete manifestation of that healing, and that's what we should do, no matter the circumstances we find ourselves in. My reaction to her also showed the headspace I was in. I was not about to accept any confession other than I was already healed (past tense). However, both can be and are true! I am already healed, and I'll continue to seek God in prayer and proclaim my healing until I see it come to completion. That's where we need to be when facing any trial. Don't confess the diagnosis more than you proclaim your healing. It doesn't deserve that much attention, power, or authority. Choose daily to magnify God over your situation. This thing was not going to take control of my life, and it most certainly wasn't going to change what I already knew God said.

Shout-out to my best friend for not only accepting my apology for how I snapped at her, but for understanding my headspace and reminding me to keep asking God until that healing completely manifested. It's so important to surround yourself with people who can not only agree with you in prayer about what we want God to do but can lovingly correct you and guide you into a better understanding of His Word! There is power in two or more (Matt. 18:19–20). We'll get to that a little later.

One last thing I want to share on this is about faith. You've got to have faith in God's Word when you face anything. I often heard the phrase, "Get God's Word in your heart," and I never really knew what that meant. I figured it meant to truly know it. Have it memorized so when the devil tries to trick you with a fake word, you'll notice it and combat it with God's Word. That's part of it, don't get me wrong, but it also means to truly believe God's Word. To know, without a doubt, that God's Word is true no matter what the doctors say, how you feel, what others say, or even what you may say at times. Despite all of that, you are healed in your heart. Man, once I got that, I was good. I made up my mind, after the disbelief about my diagnosis and the shock of it all had gone away, that I was going to stand on God's Word. I chose to believe that I was healed, without a doubt.

Now understand this: your mind may waiver. That happens because we're human. Our flesh wants to eat, and we feed it when we're constantly taking in social media and other things that can make us pay attention to things other than the truth. When we feed our flesh with this more than with God's Word, it causes us to fear and have anxiety about the very thing we're going through. How do we combat this? Submit every anxious thought to God. I have two scriptures that helped me with this:

> For the weapons of our warfare are not carnal but mighty in God for pulling down strongholds, casting down arguments and every high thing that exalts itself against the knowledge of God, bringing every thought into captivity to the obedi-

ence of Christ.

2 Corinthians 10:4–5

> Be anxious for nothing, but in everything by prayer and supplication, with thanksgiving, let your requests be made known to God; and the peace of God, which surpasses all understanding, will guard your hearts and minds through Christ Jesus.
>
> Philippians 4:6–7

Every thought that is not of God, we must bring it into the obedience of Christ. What does that look like? It means combating it with the Word. As those thoughts come across your mind, respond to those lies with the Word of God. Say, "Nope, because God says by His stripes I am already healed!" Or whatever scripture comes to mind. Sometimes I'll even say the above declaration out loud if I'm feeling it.

The second verse commands us to pray over everything and be anxious for nothing so that we may have the peace of God. I made it a habit to commit every fear, anxious thought, or feeling to God. Sometimes when I would pray and declare healing over specific things concerning my diagnosis, I would feel this small twinge of nervousness in my stomach. Instead of sitting on that, I addressed it immediately so it didn't have a chance to take root in my heart. I would say, "God, I'm not entirely sure what that feeling is from, but I surrender it to you. I am healed in Jesus' name, and You've already taken care of everything. Increase my faith!" So we must dwell on the thoughts of Jesus and not on the worries of our flesh. Those are lies of the enemy. So surrender them to the Lord and continue to know, in your heart, regardless of anything else, that you are healed.

CHAPTER 3

GOD'S WORD HEALS

"He sent His word and healed them, and delivered them from their destructions" (Ps. 107:20).

After I got over the initial shock of my diagnosis, I began to binge on healing sermons. One of my best friends sent me Dodie Osteen's testimony, and it was so powerful and encouraging. She mentions within her testimony that she read her scriptures daily. She says that she took them like medicine. I didn't realize until I started meditating on the scriptures, rotating them into my daily schedule, and making time to read them a few times a day, the power in her practice. God's Word is what sustained me throughout this whole journey. That's the battle plan! It kept me strong and stable as I faced each obstacle. I strongly believe that the only reason I was able to truly rest in Christ throughout this trial is because of His Word. It reassured me of the promises of God: I am healed!

So here is what I felt led to do, and if this resonates with you, I encourage you to try this for whatever trial you may find yourself in. I began to write down every healing scripture I was hearing. Along with listening to sermons from Kenneth Hagin and Nancy Dufresne on healing, I also found a 6-hour YouTube video of Dodie Osteen speaking healing scriptures and sharing her testimony.3 I felt led to write down every scripture she mentioned in this recording. Boy, am I glad I did that! I needed easy access to what God's Word says about me and healing. I then read these scriptures each night before bed and each morning when I woke up before I started my day.

Also, paired with this, I felt led to meditate on these scriptures. Now, meditation to me looks a little different from what other people may do. For me, meditating on His Word is talking to our Father out loud about each scripture that I read and sharing what resonated with me. Thanking Him for His Word and what it said about me. Often, this opened up a deeper conversation with the Father about situations we've gone through together and what I desired for our future. It cultivated such a beautiful atmosphere for me to be vulnerable with the Father and bask in what He's done, doing, and will do in my life. What I love about these scriptures is that they go over the standard healing scriptures (by His stripes I am healed) and also cover the authority we have in Christ Jesus. It covers the importance of having faith and not doubting, the need to assemble, and the power of agreeing together in prayer, while also sharing some healing stories like the woman with the issue of blood or the centurion man. It steps so wonderfully through all you need to know when it comes to your healing and the promises of God.

If you're interested in exactly what I studied, I've provided each scripture in the back of this book for you to review and begin speaking over yourself as you step through your trial. God's Word is so powerful and so needed when you're going through anything. What I recommend for what you're facing is to find a scripture or scriptures that speak to you and begin taking it like medicine. For me, the Lord led me to several different scriptures to meditate on. For you, He may only lead you to one or two, and that's okay. Pray about what you should meditate on and then begin taking that thing like medicine! It will be so encouraging to you as you deal with the ebbs and flows of your trial, and it truly allows you to stay stable in the Lord (1 Cor. 15:58; Col. 1:23; 2 Thess. 1:4; James 1:12).

I remember when I was given what others may see as bad news from my doctor a few weeks after my initial diagnosis, I had no fear. She told me that the cancer had spread to my lymph nodes, and I just said okay. No fear. No anxiety, because I was full of the Word and I knew what God said about my situation. I knew I was taken care of, no matter what they said. To rest in Jesus Christ is so phenomenal! You don't try to figure anything out yourself. You don't fret about what's being told to you because you know that God is faithful, and not only is He going to deliver you out of the situation, but He will strengthen you through it, and boy was I strengthened! The Lord is worthy!

CHAPTER 4

RESIST THE ENEMY

❝Therefore submit to God. Resist the devil and he will flee from you. Draw near to God and He will draw near to you. Cleanse your hands, you sinners; and purify your hearts, you double-minded" (James 4:7–8).

Whew, this sounds like such a task, right? Such a hard thing to do, especially when you're going through a trial. I'm here to tell you it's completely doable if you keep your eyes on Christ and stay rooted in God's Word. That's part of our battle plan. First, let me explain what it means. Some of you may be reading this, wondering what resisting looks like. How can I effectively resist the enemy? Well, first you need to know the enemy is prowling around like a roaring lion looking for whom he may devour:

"Be sober, be vigilant; because your adversary the devil, as a roaring lion, walketh about, seeking whom he may devour" (1 Pet. 5:8).

He is always looking for ways to kill, steal, and destroy:

"The thief does not come except to steal, and to kill, and to destroy. I have come that they may have life, and that they may have it more abundantly" (John 10:10)

The enemy wants to kill our joy, steal our peace, and destroy our confidence in the Lord. If he can do that, then we'll turn away from the Lord and seek comfort, peace, love, etc. in all the wrong places. To resist means to simply not believe the lies of the devil. What are the lies? Anything that goes against God's Word. Here's a good example: God's Word says you're healed, but your body isn't reflecting that. The enemy will try to make you think that if your body isn't showing it, you aren't healed. In your mind, he'll try to get you to entertain thoughts that question the validity of God's Word. He'll try to get you discouraged because your healing isn't reflecting in your body immediately or within your timeline. When those thoughts come, because they will, rebuke them and then speak what God's Word says. That's how Jesus defeated Satan when he tried to tempt Him on the mountain (Matt. 4:1–11).

Our minds can be the enemy's playing field. If he can get us to just entertain a lie, a thought that goes against what God has told us, then he can slowly pull us away from our Creator. To resist him means not dwelling on those thoughts, going back to God's Word, and speaking that over ourselves and our situation. I love to rebuke those thoughts out loud and speak Philippians 4:8 over myself. Then I go to scripture that declares truth and God's promises. Sometimes I'll say out loud when a lie pops up: "Nope, God's Word says that by His stripes I am healed." If you're not sure what scripture to speak, ask God. He'll show you what scripture to meditate on and combat the enemy with.

Be careful not to leave any room for the enemy to spread his lies. We do this by not entertaining any conversations, social media posts, literature, etc. that go against God's Word. Social media is one of the easiest traps the enemy can set. We're always on it.

I had to be careful not to watch videos that spoke against God's Word or showed the opposite of what I was believing God for. Sometimes I would open Instagram or TikTok and be immediately discouraged. I remember one time I opened Instagram and the first video was of a young lady who had breast cancer talking about how she was so depressed. Another time it was someone using new age, like manifesting or crystals, to heal their cancer. For me, it was no coincidence that these videos would pop up as soon as I opened those apps. I had a choice to make. I could watch that video and entertain the emotions and thoughts that came up from that, or I could skip past and declare God's Word. I wasn't perfect at this, but I did my best not to dwell on anything that didn't agree with what I was believing the Lord for. I also made it a point to listen to God's Word, praise and worship music, sermons on healing, or anything that resonated with me throughout my day while working or taking a break. This allowed me to fill up on the truth and stay full. I didn't want to provide any opportunity for the enemy to discourage me or get me off track.

Now listen, thoughts will come. That's inevitable, but what we decide to do with those thoughts is imperative. We can entertain the lies of the enemy, or we can choose to believe God's Word. Whether it's one thought or we're bombarded with thoughts, continue to fight it with truth. The enemy has already lost. It's his oldest trick in the book to try to make us not believe the promises of God. Tell him no. He doesn't get to have any room or space in your mind or your journey. Declare God's truth and stand on it. Stay so full of God's Word that the enemy has no way to get in. I once heard during a sermon that if you resist the enemy well, he'll flee from you well. Let's be great resisters!

CHAPTER 5

YOUR BODY DOESN'T DICTATE YOUR HEALING

This lesson, I believe, is one of the biggest lessons you can learn when going through your healing journey. For me, in the past, I just knew I was healed if my body showed it. I wanted instant healing too. Just like the people that you see so many times in the Bible. I wanted it to happen quickly and I wanted my body to show it immediately. Ya'll, I'm here to tell you that our healing is not dictated by whether our body shows it or not. It's not, "By His stripes and when my body shows it, I'm healed." It's by His stripes I am healed. Just because your body isn't reflecting it yet doesn't make it any less true. Once I wrapped my head around that, it made my journey so much easier because I knew that even though my body didn't reflect it yet, it would.

In one of the sermons I watched on healing, the preacher said, "Don't check your body— check the Word." So good! Checking your body every day to see if the healing is manifesting in physical form is a lot and can be discouraging if you're not seeing or feeling any change when you feel like you should. This is why our bodies cannot be the signifier of if we're healed. God's Word has to always be what we stand on. I learned to just believe I was healed. In my prayer time, I would say, "God, Your Word says, by Your stripes I am healed. I believe that and I receive that, regardless of what my body is doing, how I may feel, what others say, or what I may say.

I declare that I am healed." Your body will bow to that truth.

In Abraham and Sarah's story, God told them that they would bear a child. Both Abraham and Sarah were past the age the world said they could have a child. I say "the world said" because the world will have you believe that God can't make something like that happen because they're too old. Know this: there is nothing impossible for God, and if He promises they will conceive, even in their nineties, then it is so. In one of the verses, it says that Abraham did not consider his own body or the deadness of Sarah's womb; he believed what God promised:

> And not being weak in faith, he did not consider his own body, already dead (since he was about a hundred years old), and the deadness of Sarah's womb. He did not waver at the promise of God through unbelief, but was strengthened in faith, giving glory to God, and being fully convinced that what He had promised He was also able to perform.
> Romans 4:19–21

That is exactly the mindset we must have. Let's not consider our bodies because that will discourage you. Let's stand on God's promise that we are already healed. If we believe it and speak it over ourselves, over our children's bodies, and over our situations, then those things have to line up:

"It is the same with my word. I send it out, and it always produces fruit. It will accomplish all I want it to, and it will prosper everywhere I send it" (Isa. 55:11, NLT).

God's Word always does what it says it's going to do. So if we're declaring it over our situations, it will eventually line up. However, don't wait for your body to line up to believe it. Believe it despite what your body is doing. Now, I want to say here that if you've spoken God's Word over your situation and nothing is lining up, then a few things could be going on here. The first is that you don't have the faith to believe the Word. So you're speaking it with no faith attached. Without faith, God's Word can't do what it needs to do (Matt. 21:21–22; Mark 11:22–24). So faith is required and is so powerful. Check your faith.

Secondly, it could be that you're too focused on your timeline and expecting God to move in a timetable that makes sense to you. Stop putting God in a box and trust His timing. Just because it's not happening in your timing does not mean God is not moving. Trust Him!

Thirdly, it could be that there is some unforgiveness or sin that you haven't dealt with yet. So God needs you to address this before He can move in this situation. Exodus 15:26 and Exodus 23:25 both address that God will take away sickness from those who serve the Lord, diligently heed His voice, and do what's right in His sight. Our healing is tied to our obedience. So, go to the Father and ask Him to shed light on any area of your life where you've disobeyed Him or any area that is stopping your healing from fully manifesting within your body and repent.

Lastly, it could be something outside of what I mentioned going on. For all of these, seek the Father and be open to what He has to say. He'll show you where you land. God's Word always moves and never fails (Josh. 21:45; 1 Kings 8:56), so if it isn't moving in our situation, it's us and not God. He's done everything needed for us to walk in healing. We must stand on that and take authority over our healing. All in all, commune with God and He'll give you wisdom:

"If any of you lacks wisdom, let him ask of God, who gives to all liberally and without reproach, and it will be given to him" (James 1:5).

He wants to give wisdom to His people so that we can walk confidently in our authority. God is not in the business of hiding anything from us. So remember, your body does not dictate God's healing—His Word does, and according to His Word, we are already healed. Let us walk confidently in His promises!

CHAPTER 6

PRAY FERVENTLY

Prayer is one of the most important things that you can do throughout your lifetime. Oftentimes, we see people coming to the Father in desperation through prayer. They treat God as a last resort when things are not going well in their lives and they've hit a wall. They no longer have control of the situation, and all options have gone. However, God requires us to commune with Him daily (Heb. 4:16). Our Father is not just an "in crisis God." He is an "all-the-time God." We need to meet with Him daily and allow Him to speak to our hearts, encouraging us, loving us, providing wisdom and comfort, and just simply sharing what He has for us. When going through a trial, prayer is even more important. Our desire to converse with God needs to grow, but also how often we connect with Him as we step through the trial needs to increase because we truly do need Him.

The definition of fervently is "very enthusiastically or passionately."[4] To pray fervently is to pray with enthusiasm and with passion toward our Father. I'll take it even deeper. The definition of enthusiasm, or to do something enthusiastically, is "showing intense and eager enjoyment, interest, or approval."[5] We must pray intensely, with eager enjoyment and interest, to our Father. The Word tells us:

"The effective, fervent prayer of a righteous man avails [benefits/ helps] much" (James 5:16).

It is to our benefit to pray fervently. Part of the strategy that God gave me when I was first diagnosed was connecting with Him in prayer each morning and each night. I was doing this my way before, but not fervently and specific to anything most days. Just that general prayer to watch over my family, forgive me of my sins, and grow me in the Father. My strategy had to change. I had to declare God's Word over my life. I said, "God, Your Word says that by Your stripes, I am healed. So I declare that I am healed from the top of my head to the soles of my feet." I began to rebuke the spirit of cancer, the spirit of sickness and infirmity over my life. I would speak to those spirits and tell them they had no power and cast them into the pit of hell. I would pray specifically for the things I was told about my condition and pray the exact opposite of that. If they said my counts were low in a particular area or I had infected tissue, I would declare that those counts come up in Jesus' name. I would say that there was no infected tissue, only healthy tissue in the name of Jesus. We have the authority to declare these things in the name of Jesus (Mark 16:17–18). Take your authority and declare God's truth! The Lord will reveal to you what to pray specifically. Begin with just speaking God's Word over your life and over your situation and declaring that alone.

Over time, the Lord will lead you to specific things. He'll give you insight and wisdom on what to continue to pray. His Word says that He gives wisdom generously (James 1:5); we just have to ask for it. Next, we need to praise God that it is already done. As I mentioned in the last chapter, our bodies or circumstances do not dictate if we receive healing. Healing is ours. It became ours when Christ took stripes for it on the Cross. So, let's thank God for healing our bodies. Let's thank God that it is already done, even if we don't see it yet.

I began to pray each morning and night, declaring my healing and speaking God's Word. Throughout the day, as things came up, I'd pray over those things as well. If fear surfaced about something or anxiety began to show its ugly head over something I read or saw or just my thoughts, I surrendered that to the Lord. One of the things I learned is to not sit with feelings of fear, worry, or uneasiness. As soon as those feelings that are not of the Lord came up, I'd address them with God immediately. I did not give those feelings a chance to take root in my mind and cause any harm. I took them to God. I asked the Father where these came from. I repented for them and then I surrendered it to the Lord. This is also a great way to resist the enemy. He'll try to implant thoughts that are a hundred percent lies. As soon as it surfaces in our minds, we must rebuke it and give it over to God to deal with. We don't want anything that isn't from the Father taking root in our minds, gaining power, and effecting our walk. We must be intentional about entertaining God-breathed thoughts and truth and truth alone. The enemy doesn't get to run rampant in our minds. That's giving him too much power, and he isn't owed that because he's already defeated!

"Behold, I give you the authority to trample on serpents and scorpions, and over all the power of the enemy, and nothing shall by any means hurt you" (Luke 10:19).

CHAPTER 7

REJOICE, IT'S A TRIAL!

Gosh, how bizarre is it to rejoice during a trial? I would hear this and think, "What? How can I rejoice? A trial is not easy!" However, the Bible calls us to rejoice. Why? To rejoice increases our endurance:

"My brethren, count it all joy when you fall into various trials, knowing that the testing of your faith produces patience. But let patience have its perfect work, that you may be perfect and complete, lacking nothing" (James 1:2–4).

I found this idea so difficult to wrap my head around in the past. I would pray for it because the Word says it, but I truly didn't understand it. I would even declare that I'd rejoice and try to see the lighter, joyful side of the trial I was facing. However, I never felt it. I never actually rejoiced truly, until now. So what changed? I stayed rooted in God's Word and I stayed connected to the Father in prayer. I know I've said that constantly throughout this text, but it is so true and so powerful! That's the battle plan! To stay rooted in God's Word and connected to Him.

What I neglected to do in the past was find scripture that spoke to my situation and declare it over myself, the people I loved, or my circumstances. I didn't speak to the Father regularly about the trial and declare His Word in my life. Most importantly, I didn't have enough faith that my situation would change. Gosh, that's hard to write, but it's so true. Going through this trial highlighted the lack of faith I had in the past because I was stagnant in seeking the Father and declaring His Word. I would pray about the situation a few times and kind of just leave it at that, and eventually, over time, it would change, but I'd struggle through it.

When I found out the diagnosis, I had a decision to make: go through this with God or without Him. I chose to go through it with Him because, honestly, I had no idea how to do it otherwise. When I chose Him, He downloaded a battle plan into my heart rooted in His Word. That's what the scripture at the beginning of this book references. I had to see His Word, get it in my heart by believing it without a doubt, commune with the Father daily, and declare His Word over myself and my circumstances. Anytime I felt fear or doubt or anything that went against what God's Word told me, I gave it over to the Father and we dealt with it together. I have to say, as I stayed consistent here, I got excited to see what God was doing and was about to do in my current circumstances. I was excited to grow closer to the Father and truly know Him as a healer. I was able to rejoice because I knew, regardless of what the enemy tried to make me believe or what the doctors said, I was good. I felt an inner peace and joy because I knew the Father had me, and it was so refreshing. To truly rest in God's Word and have confidence knowing the promise has to perform was such a magnificent feeling! God doesn't lie. I was just so excited for what God was about to do.

So how did God move in my situation? Great question! The first thing that comes to mind is His daily strength. His Word says:

"But those who wait on the Lord shall renew their strength; they shall mount up with wings like eagles, they shall run and not be weary, they shall walk and not faint" (

Each day, He gave me the power to go on and face the day. He eliminated the negative reaction I would have had to treatment. I had minimal to no symptoms. I could function well daily, so much so that I was able to still work during treatment. Although I lost my hair because of the chemotherapy, God managed to turn that into a joyful experience. To lose my hair was one of the scariest things for me and I didn't want to face it. I dreaded it and prayed, begged, pleaded, and declared that it wouldn't fall out during treatment. That, however, was not the case. When I began to see my hair fall out, I've got to admit, your girl freaked out. It was just a huge shock to see my beautiful, kinky, curly hair in my hands. I saw that and I broke down. Although my mom and sister comforted me, I was just so upset. It took almost the whole day for me to talk to the Lord about it. I sat in my sad feelings for most of the day, not talking to anyone. Can I share something with you? God cares about the things we care about and He collects our tears: "Casting all your care upon Him, for He cares for you" (1 Pet. 5:7).

"You number my wanderings; Put my tears into Your bottle; are they not in Your book?" (Psa. 56:8).

He doesn't like to see us suffer, and one of the things we often don't realize is that our Father is going through this trial with us. He never leaves us or forsakes us (Deut. 31:6 8). He is right there walking through it with us and encouraging us to give it over to Him:

"Cast your burden on the Lord, and He shall sustain you; He shall never permit the righteous to be moved" (Psa. 55:22).

Finally, that night, I talked to God about it. I decided to just be honest about how upset and disappointed I was. I poured out to Him all the things I felt. After a hefty venting session, the Lord began to reassure me that this was not that bad. This was temporary, and just as He strengthened me through the ups and downs of treatment, He's got me here. I felt lighter. All of a sudden, what felt like the worst thing in the world became a fun thing. That next day, my dad shaved my head. Although my family was in shock at the change, I was excited to see myself bald and feel areas of my head I hadn't seen before. I was also excited to try on wigs and switch it up for a bit. God truly changed my perspective, and I couldn't have been more grateful.

Lastly, I'll share that God truly had His hand on the nurses and doctors in charge of my care. Some were believers themselves, and I could talk to them about what God was doing in this journey. Each person I came across truly cared about my treatment and wanted me to get well. His hands were on my labs and scans. Each week, when my labs came back from treatment, they always looked great. Any scans I had to get to check if the cancer had spread or if there was something wrong in another area of my body always came back clear and clean. Finally, if we did find that my counts from one of my labs were too high or too low, once I prayed about it and surrendered it to the Father, it would regulate and I'd be in the clear. Our Father is so awesome, and He moves on behalf of His people!

CHAPTER 8

SHARE YOUR TESTIMONY, DON'T WAIT!

Okay, so I'm shouting this part from the rooftops. Share, share, SHARE, your testimony as much as possible!

"And they overcame him by the blood of the Lamb and by the word of their testimony, and they did not love their lives to the death" (Rev. 12:11).

"I shall not die but live, and declare the works of the Lord" (Psa. 118:17).

Why? Because the Word tells us to and it not only encourages others who are watching you but it encourages you. It forces you to look back on what God did and remember that if He did it for me through that trial, He can do it again! Oh, and get this, you don't have to wait to share when the trial is over. Share when you're right, smack dab, in the middle of it! Let's worship the Father before we get to the end of the thing as if it's already done:

"And in that day you will say: 'Praise the Lord, call upon His name; declare His deeds among the peoples, make mention that His name is exalted. Sing to the Lord, for He has done excellent things; this is known in all the earth'" (Isa. 12:4–5).

Sharing our testimony while we are in the middle of the storm cultivates an atmosphere of praise toward the Father. It not only allows us to remember what God is doing and will do but forces us to praise Him as we go through. What I also love about sharing your testimony in the middle of it is that it shows others that it's okay to give God praise before we see the promise come through fully. God is still working things out, but we'll still honor Him. We're in the middle of it, but we'll give God the praise while we wait for Him to complete what He's started in us:

"Being confident of this very thing, that He who has begun a good work in you will complete it until the day of Jesus Christ" (Phil. 1:6).

This should give us confidence that our Father completes everything He starts. So, as God opens up opportunities for you to share your testimony, take it. For some of us, He's asked us to wait a bit before sharing it with everyone all at once. He may pick a select few to start with. That was my story. I didn't feel led to tell everyone all at once what I was going through as I was going through it. I believe the Father truly wanted me to stay focused on what He tasked me to do during the trial, and He didn't want me to complicate that process by trying to manage other people's opinions or projected fears of my situation. Which I completely get, and I'm so grateful for because, knowing me, I would struggle with trying to please everyone and not the Father.

However, during the trial, the Lord placed it on my heart whom I could tell, and cultivated situations for me to share with others. He was strategic about whom to share with as I walked through this journey. I was able to share what I learned up to that point and what the Lord was doing within my body and with my family. I just felt a sense of peace and knew it was okay to share this part of my story with some. He also showed me when it was time to share this part of my story with you all. So stay connected to Him. He'll give you the okay when to share and with whom.

Remember that the enemy doesn't want us to share our testimony. So he'll try to convince you to stay quiet about it. Whether that's through shame, fear, or anxiety. Don't let him win in that area. If you feel led to share your testimony with someone or a group of people, do it! Let the enemy know that you are not afraid to talk about what God is doing in your life. This is so important because it will strengthen you to keep going. It will also encourage those who may be going through the same thing or a different trial of their own. We never know how choosing to be transparent about our testimony can help others who need to be reminded that God still heals or that He still moves even in the craziest of situations.

When you're going through a long trial it can get exhausting. You may get to a point where you are just tired of stepping through it. There may be a lot coming at you. When you are constantly ready to share your testimony as God allows, this encourages you to keep going by forcing you to think about how mighty our God is and how He's gotten you through so far. That's such a beautiful thing! So, share the mess out of your testimony and trust God as he provides you with opportunities to do it.

CHAPTER 9

YOU HAVE AUTHORITY

Can I share something so beautiful with you? To know the authority that you have in the Lord is one of the best weapons you'll have. Knowing your authority is powerful and can help you navigate any season you're in. Why? Because you're not just going to stand for the tricks of the enemy. If it's not of the Lord, it has to go. This gave me such a boost and raised such a fight in me when I got it. I wasn't just going to take what the enemy threw at me. Here are two verses I meditated on:

> And these signs will follow those who believe: In My name, they will cast out demons; they will speak with new tongues; they will take up serpents; and if they drink anything deadly, it will by no means hurt them; they will lay hands on the sick, and they will recover.
> Mark 16:17–18

> Behold, I give you the authority to trample on serpents and scorpions, and over all the power of the enemy, and nothing shall by any means hurt you.
> Luke 10:19

Look at the power we have in Christ. We can cast out demons, take up serpents, lay hands on the sick, speak in new tongues, and the enemy cannot hurt us. Sometimes we feel like we need to have the pastor or an elder pray for us because maybe we think they have more authority. That's what I thought. I used to think that the prayers of those who went to church their whole lives, or anyone who seemed more mature in the Word than myself would get answered before mine. That's such a lie the enemy wants us to believe to keep us from growing, taking our authority, and having a personal relationship with the Father. The Word says in Jesus' name we have authority. We don't have to wait for an elder or pastor to pray over us or command healing—we have the power to do it ourselves.

Now, don't get me wrong, there is nothing wrong with having an elder of your church, your pastor, grandma, or whoever believes God's Word to pray for you. The more prayer, the better, and sometimes we need their faith to help boost our faith and keep us on track. I get it. I'm simply saying we have the power ourselves to command healing and rebuke sickness. As long as we have the faith to believe, it shall be so.

> So Jesus answered and said to them, "Assuredly, I say to you, if you have faith and do not doubt, you will not only do what was done to the fig tree, but also if you say to this mountain, 'Be removed and be cast into the sea,' it will be done. And whatever things you ask in prayer, believing, you will receive."
> Matthew 21:21–22

The scripture tells us that if we have faith and do not doubt, whatever we ask, if we believe, we shall have it. How awesome is that! We can tell that mountain to go and it has to bow. Your mountain could be sickness, poverty, debt, addiction, fear, anxiety, etc. Whatever the enemy has tried to attack you with to keep you from growing in the Lord. Anything that has kept you bound. You don't have to just deal with it. You have the power to speak to that mountain and command it to go in the mighty name of Jesus. When I say that God's Word is my strength, this is what I mean.

When I was meditating on God's Word, I got so many mighty revelations over scriptures I've read before and heard over and over again. To truly understand my authority strengthened me. To learn that healing is already mine strengthened me. It's a promise of God, and to know it's not something I have to try to get or beg for strengthened me. To discover the power of agreement when two or more come together and agree that they, not only can have whatever they ask, but God is in the midst, that strengthened me. I could go on, but simply put, God's Word is our strength, and it is so important to stay connected to it always, especially during a trial.

One last thing I want to share with you about this and that is speaking to your body or your symptoms and commanding them to go. What I found was that I could easily speak to the spirit of cancer and sickness and command it to go, but when it came to the symptoms of the chemo and some side effects that I had, I just accepted them. Sometimes, it felt like a chore to speak to the small things. I always thought that was so bizarre that I could pray for the big things and command those to go but for the smaller things, for whatever reason, I didn't have the energy. Well, first of all, it's a flesh issue, and I think that is a way for us to self-sabotage. We think, or at least I did at times, that just because it's a small symptom, I can just deal with it. Nope. Muster up the energy and bind those small symptoms just as you did the big sickness. I also think it's just like the enemy to make us think that the small symptoms are nothing and we are just too tired to command them to go. Absolutely not! We want total freedom. Speak to EVERY SINGLE THING!

The sickness and every single symptom that comes with it and believe, without doubt, that those things have to go.

You might be saying, "Well, Janeé, I read your book from the beginning, and I saw that you prayed about not losing your hair, and you still did. What about that?" Well, first I'd say, nice catch! Thanks for paying attention to my story, ha! Secondly, I'd say, you're right. I did pray about that particular side effect and it still happened. However, I was obsessed with not losing my hair. You can say that I almost made an idol out of it. It was no longer about trusting God's plan for me in this journey but about getting my way. Not only did I not want my hair to fall out, but I wanted this thing over quickly. I had it set in my mind how this trial was going to go.

You see, the problem with that mindset is that God is no longer in control—I am. He never calls us to take control. He calls us to just cast our cares over to Him. It was never my job to steer the Lord in my journey. It was always my job to rest in Him and trust Him as we stepped through each phase. I believe that God allowed my hair to fall out to show me that even in this, He can strengthen me. Even in this, I am victorious. Now, everyone's journey is different and He'll do it differently for you versus how He did it for me. However, always know that God's plans for you are good, and He doesn't want us to suffer or go through the trial without Him. Invite Him in and watch Him strengthen you through the ups and downs of the trial. It's a beautiful process.

CHAPTER 10

LISTEN, SPEAK, BELIEVE

"So then faith comes by hearing, and hearing by the word of God" (Rom. 10:17).

When I began my journey, one of the first things I did was find a YouTube video that spoke the healing scriptures so that I could listen as much as possible. I knew that God's Word was healing, and I wanted it going in my ear as much as possible. One, because if I'm listening to God's Word I don't have time to entertain thoughts of the flesh (fear, doubt, lies of the enemy, etc.). Secondly, I wanted my faith to increase, and I knew if I started listening to what God's Word said about healing it would get my faith up. Faith comes by hearing (Rom. 10:17)! Little did I know that was the first step to increasing my faith.

The next step would be to meditate on God's Word constantly. So, I found a 6-hour video of Dodie Osteen reciting healing scriptures and sharing her testimony that looped throughout my day. I loved it! I would play this every day, in the background, while I worked. Although I had heard these sayings over and over again, I would still get so riled up when I would hear certain scriptures. It was just so renewing and refreshing to hear what God's Word has to say about me. I never got tired of hearing it because it was doing something on the inside of me to help me fight this fight. It got me excited to see God's hand moving in my life. So, start listening to God's Word more consistently. It'll help you stay full on God's Word.

Next, speak to that thing. Life and death are in the power

of the tongue (Prov. 18:21). What you proclaim over yourself is powerful. Some of us stay bound up in sickness, depression, fear, and anxiety because we are declaring that we are those things and not declaring God's Word. Nope! Let's start speaking God's Word, truth, powerful truth, over ourselves and our circumstances. Let's not identify with the enemy's attacks but identify with the mighty Word of God.

Declare this with me: "I am healed, restored, and made whole! Sickness, you have no authority! I am a child of God, and God's Word for His children is that by His stripes we are healed. So I am healed. I believe it and receive it, no matter what my body is doing, what I see, what others say, or even what I may say. I am healed, in the mighty name of Jesus. I speak to the spirit of... (insert the sickness you're battling here—mine was cancer), sickness, ailment, and disease, and I bind you in the mighty name of Jesus. I renounce your power in Jesus' name. You have no power, authority, or dominion in the name of Jesus. I cast you into the pit of hell in Jesus' name, and I loose healing, wholeness, and restoration from the top of my head to the soles of my feet in the mighty name of Jesus!"

Declare that over yourself. God's Word is power, and what we speak over ourselves is powerful. That sickness is trespassing; let's not give it any power. We must let that spirit know, the moment it tries to pop up, that it has no authority and it's not staying long. That thing is trespassing because we are healed in Jesus' name!

Now, let's tie it all together with belief. None of this works if we don't believe what God's Word says about us. We must have the faith to anchor this on. Read what God's Word says about your circumstances and you. Keep meditating on that thing until you believe it without a doubt. For me, something just clicked. I was not willing to entertain anything other than what God's Word said about me. I didn't just have to deal with what the doctors told me. I didn't just have to receive it. Oh, no, I could go back to my very Creator, give this situation to Him, declare what He says about me over my situation, and choose to stand on that, regardless of what I was told.

Remember my story above? When I went to the doctor, they told me that the cancer had spread to my lymph nodes. I was so full of God's Word that it didn't even phase me. It didn't matter what I was told. I was already healed, and I knew that it was only a matter of time before my body submitted to that truth. So, the doctor told me, and I said, "Okay! I feel good!" I know she thought I was crazy, but when you know, you know. God had me. My circumstances didn't matter. So stand on God's Word and believe that what He said He's going to do, He will do. He is not a man that He should lie (Num. 23:19), and His promises never fail (1 Kings 8:56)!

CHAPTER 11

CONCERN LIST

Can I encourage you today to make a list of things that you want to see healed in your healing journey? As I mentioned above, it was easy to pray about the big sickness, cancer, but harder to pray about the smaller symptoms I was experiencing. I think I had a bit of tunnel vision to only focus on the bigger picture and not exactly the smaller symptoms from the chemo treatment or the medication I was on. However, God wants all of it. Yes, get specific about your diagnosis, but submit those side effects, reactions to medications, and small things that changed over to Christ as well. He wants it all. His Word says to cast your cares unto the Lord—not to cast your big cares only. He wants everything. So I began to write down my concerns to keep me on track with all that I was experiencing. This list also helped me to know what to continue to pray for as I stepped through this journey. God's Word says that He will perfect our concerns:

"The Lord will perfect that which concerns me; Your mercy, O Lord, endures forever; do not forsake the works of Your hands" (Psa. 138:8).

I wanted a record of the things He perfected in my life. So, I wrote them down as they came up. Now, I can't take credit for this idea. I heard it first from Dodie Osteen, and I thought it was so clever, so I began to do it myself. It helped me to keep track of everything and know what to pray for. It also acted as a memorial of what God had done. I can always look back at that list years from now and see how God healed me.

Your list doesn't have to be fancy. For me, it was just a note on my phone titled Concern List. I added the verse at the beginning of this chapter at the top of the note. Then I made a running list of all the things I wanted healed. From no nausea or fatigue from the chemo to all new breast tissue with no trace of cancer to be found. As I saw these different things come to fruition, I would cross them off my list. I also began to document my overall victories in healing, not just concerning the cancer. For example, I remember waking up one morning with some back pain. I laid hands on my back, declared healing, and commanded the pain to go, and by the end of the day it was gone. I documented that with the date and praised God for it. So those types of victories went in too.

I also added certain battles that the Lord gave me victory over. I shared with you earlier that losing my hair was a fear of mine. I zoomed in on praying that I wouldn't lose it and commanding my follicles to stay. However, my hair did fall out. I documented when it fell out and that God gave me the victory over this mountain. I celebrated the victory and how God came through. That was important to me to see the thing I feared turn into a victory and a fun encounter. Every time I read it, it makes me happy to see God's hand in that situation.

So make yourself a list. Start with the diagnosis you were given and you can write that you want your body to be rid of this sickness completely. Then start to get specific. Everything that the doctors told me that was wrong within my body, I wrote down as something to be corrected. For instance, they shared that my estrogen and progesterone levels were high, so I wrote that those levels would come back down to a healthy and normal level. If they say certain cells are high or certain areas are swollen, write those down as things to be normalized or healed, and as you see God do it, add the date it was done and cross it off your list. If you want, add other victories to your list, like I did, outside of your big diagnosis as a way to track victory in your life. It is encouraging to look back and see the hand of God move, especially as you enter your next trial. You'll have this list to look back on and motivate you to not grow weary.

CHAPTER 12

COMMUNITY IS EVERYTHING

One of the things that I was most grateful for as I went through this healing journey was how I was surrounded by loved ones who encouraged me along the way. I mentioned above that I didn't tell everybody all at once when I was given the diagnosis of breast cancer. One, because it was extremely hard to share the diagnosis over and over again with loved ones and see their reactions. Secondly, once I had my mind set on total healing, without a doubt, I needed to surround myself with people who believed God for the same things and nothing less. Over time, I shared with more loved ones, and I made sure I had a community of people who I could come together and pray with because there is power in agreement.

"Again I say to you that if two of you agree on earth concerning anything that they ask, it will be done for them by My Father in heaven. For where two or three are gathered together in My name, I am there in the midst of them" (Matt. 18:19–20).

It's so important that you have people in your corner who you can agree with and declare God's Word. People who can still stand on the Word when you struggle and ask God for the miraculous and impossible on your behalf. That is so important because it teaches you to not put God in a box and reminds you that we serve a God of the impossible. So, ask big, and when you can't, your community can. Family who can pray for what you are believing God for and more. Intercessors and fighters who can war in the spirit for you as you step through your trial. It's so refreshing! To have people in your corner ready to pray when you need them or speak encouragement in your life is a wonderful thing. So get you a tribe. Don't think about going through this alone, but ask God to send you people who can pray with you, for you, and believe God with you on your healing. It's a relief to know that you don't have to go through this by yourself. I not only had a great group of prayer warriors around me, but I was rooted in a great church that believed in healing and declared it over my life as I stepped through it.

CHAPTER 13

GOD FINISHES WHAT HE STARTS

When you step back and examine my testimony, it's easy to label the entire thing as one big mountain, and it certainly was. However, there were little mountains within this journey that I was stepping through. One was my surgery. There was a lot of talk from my doctors about doing a mastectomy because the cancer they found was big and it put me at stage three. The word mastectomy alone scared me because I was only thirty-three. I didn't want to have such a major surgery at such a young age. So, I began to pray about it and give it over to the Lord. Now, if I'm honest, I'll say that my will got in the way here just a little bit in the beginning. When I prayed, I did more telling God what I wanted to happen versus desiring His way. Sometimes you can get so wrapped up in what makes sense to you and how you want to share your testimony that you forget that God is the author of that and not us. I could tell that the Lord was working on my heart with that because I began to feel convicted about telling God what I wanted instead of asking Him what He wanted and praying for His desires.

As we got closer to surgery time, I could tell my heart shifted a bit about my plans. I knew that God was giving me a new perspective, just like He did when I lost my hair. I became more accepting of whatever He wanted, even if it was completely different from what I wanted. I knew whatever happened, I would be okay because our Father was in control.

So, the surgery happened, it went extremely well, and I had the mastectomy. Yup, I had the mastectomy and I was fine. Just like God told me I would be.

As time went on and discouragement tried to slide in, I wouldn't let it. I reminded myself that God's will was better than mine for anything. He made me excited about what was next to come. His way is so much better than mine and it considers things and people we just don't have the capacity or knowledge to consider. To me, that's such a precious thing.

So, I've had the surgery, and we've pushed past such a big mountain, and for a second there it felt like things slowed down. There were things I was still praying for, and it just felt like we were at a pause. I even considered stopping my scriptures because it felt like we were at the end of the journey. I'm here to tell you that your journey is not complete until your healing is complete. God doesn't do half the job and walk away. He is faithful to FINISH what He started:

"Being confident of this very thing, that He who has begun a good work in you will complete it until the day of Jesus Christ" (Phil. 1:6).

Yes, the surgery was a mighty mountain, but so were the other things I was believing God for. So I continued to press. I continued to declare healing and rebuke other symptoms and ailments that were happening in my body. I want to be totally restored and completely healed. Just because it doesn't feel like God is moving does not mean He isn't. He wants to know, are we still going to pursue Him even for the other things, or will we quit because it's taking too long? I stayed on it as things on my concern list that I was believing God for were answered. We serve a mighty God! Stay on it and continue to press. He will complete what He began!

CHAPTER 14

MY FULL TESTIMONY

Although I've referenced different aspects of my testimony throughout this book, I wanted to provide it to you fully here in one place. I think it's important to share what I went through and how God provided. You see it through these chapters, but let me condense it here for you just a bit.

At the end of May 2023, I felt a lump in my right breast. At first, I thought it could be just something non-serious, like hard tissue or cartilage. I didn't want to worry and make it into a huge issue. So I tried to put it out of my mind for a while, but the Holy Spirit kept bringing it up to me. Eventually, I decided to tell my primary doctor about it at my next appointment. Mind you, I felt this in May, and my next check-up wasn't until July. Even though I decided to wait until July to get it checked, I still felt uneasiness and, now that I think about it, a haste or urgency to get checked a lot sooner than that. When I attempted to reschedule with my doctor to an earlier date, she didn't have anything available until October. So I kept my current appointment. The next day or so, I felt the need to check again. I did, and my doctor had something available that day (come on, Holy Spirit!). I rescheduled immediately and went in to see her.

Although I was able to secure an appointment with her, the challenge wasn't over. I still had to work up the courage to say something. On one hand, I felt like she would dismiss me because it was a busy day at the doctor's office and she hadn't been too personable, and let's be honest, I wasn't even sure about what I felt. So, I explained my reason for my checkup (as I had a few other things I wanted advice/direction on), and at the end of my very short list, I mentioned the lump I felt in my right breast. She didn't say anything immediately, just asked me to hop on the exam table to begin my check-up. When she felt the area of concern, she told me that it didn't feel like what a lump in the breast would feel like but that she'd order me a mammogram. There was a sigh of relief and concern, but I didn't want to worry.

The next week, I went in for my mammogram, and a mass was found. Again, I didn't want to worry because honestly, when they told me, I don't think I really took in the news or truly understood what finding a mass meant. I was told not to worry because it could be anything, not just cancer. I then went back into that same treatment center a few days later for a biopsy that they would send to pathology to see what exactly we were looking at. I want to pause and say that God's hand was moving here, too! Not only did the Holy Spirit urge me to get the lump checked out and made a way by opening a slot for me to talk to my doctor as soon as possible, but I had the sweetest nurses and techs when I went to get my mammogram and biopsy. They were all so compassionate and kind. It's like God was pouring out His love through these people before I even found out what I was dealing with.

Once I got everything done, it took a few days before I heard back. I got the call from the doctor, and it was indeed breast cancer. My doctor told me the news and that a breast surgeon would follow up with me in a few days. Again, I couldn't believe it. Even as I told my parents and sister, I couldn't even call it breast cancer. Just a clump of cancer cells. That description was all I could mentally handle.

Our meeting with the breast surgeon was about a week later, and this is when things became real. She walked through the type of cancer they found. She explained what caused it and how long she thought the mass was there, as well as the treatment plan, which included chemotherapy, surgery, and radiation. In that order. My heart sank. I could not believe I was dealing with a cancer diagnosis. How could this happen so soon after my uncle's funeral? The uncle who passed away fighting leukemia. Tears swelled in my eyes as she continued to explain the next steps. I tried to wrap my head around what my life would look like over the next few weeks. Even here, I felt God's love. The first thing my breast surgeon said to me when she walked in was that we would fight this. I would be okay. Look at God being an encourager!

Telling my immediate family was the next part, and this was going to be hard because I knew the moment I talked about it, I would break down. We got home, gathered my mother and sister, and I fought through tears as I shared the news. I let out everything. My parents and sister held my hand, patted me on the back, and tried to stay strong as I dealt with what I heard. This is when my mom turned to me and said, "We've got to fight," and fight we did indeed!

I told two of my best friends, along with my pastor and first lady, that I had these tests done, and on the prayer line that week my first lady asked me if everything turned out okay. I told her the news, and the moment prayer was over, she asked a few ladies to stay on the line to pray for me. Before she began to pray, she encouraged me and told me that God has me and I'm healed. She told me to no longer shed tears of fear or worry over this because I was covered. My friends on the line expressed the same sentiments, and my first lady led us into prayer. God showed His hand here again. To me, He was saying, "Daughter, I have you! I've surrounded you with people who love you and will war in the spirit with you and for you. I've surrounded you with people who will encourage you when you need it. You are covered, my sweet girl." How I love the Father.

The next few months were full of scans, tests, surgery, and chats with different doctors and nurses who would be on my team, leading my treatment and setting up appointments. It was a lot! However, during that time I was also getting full on God's Word. The battle plan! I was speaking healing scriptures over myself and rebuking cancer in Jesus' name. I was learning about the authority I have and how Jesus has done everything He needs on this earth for our healing when He died on the Cross. It was now up to me to walk in the authority He's given us as believers and claim my healing. I was already healed. I walk through this more specifically in the chapters above, but man, I was so excited to watch God's hand move in this journey. Joy and peace surrounded me and excitement bubbled inside of me. God truly moved!

I can excitedly say that as I write this, I am cancer-free! I received this update on January 26, 2024. Not only did God do it, but He kept me in awe throughout the entire process. Although I still have preventative treatment to come, just as He strengthened me before, He will again through this next phase. I am so excited to continue to watch God's hand move.

I hope what I've shared in the chapters above and here within my full testimony encourages you. I hope it reminds you that whether you're dealing with sickness or anything else, the Father has you. The Father loves you, and if you are willing to surrender to Him, He will take care of everything better than you can imagine. Praise God. Jehovah Rapha (God, my healer)!

CHAPTER 15

HEALING SCRIPTURES

Below are the healing scriptures I stepped through and meditated on as I was going through my trial. I share them with you in hopes that it will be a blessing as you face the storms ahead. Remember, this is your medicine. So, take as needed. I recommend a dosage of as much as possible, to be taken daily. Consult with the Father on what scriptures you should meditate on. Follow the leading of the Holy Spirit as you walk through the Word and pause on the scriptures He's placed on your heart. Allow His Word to wash over you and strengthen you as you step through your trial daily.

- Exodus 15:26

    - And said, "If you diligently heed the voice of the Lord your God and do what is right in His sight, give ear to His commandments and keep all His statutes, I will put none of the diseases on you which I have brought on the Egyptians. For I am the Lord who heals you."

- Exodus 23:25

    - So you shall serve the Lord your God, and He will bless your bread and your water. And I will take sickness away from the midst of you.

- Deuteronomy 7:15

    - And the Lord will take away from you all

sickness, and will afflict you with none of the terrible diseases of Egypt which you have known, but will lay them on all those who hate you.

- Deuteronomy 28:1–2

    - Now it shall come to pass, if you diligently obey the voice of the Lord your God, to observe carefully all His commandments which I command you today, that the Lord your God will set you high above all nations of the earth. And all these blessings shall come upon you and overtake you, because you obey the voice of the Lord your God.

- Deuteronomy 30:19

    - I call heaven and earth as witnesses today against you, that I have set before you life and death, blessing and cursing; therefore choose life, that both you and your descendants may live.

- Joshua 21:45

    - Not a word failed of any good thing which the Lord had spoken to the house of Israel. All came to pass.

- 1 Kings 8:56

    - Blessed be the Lord, who has given rest to His people Israel, according to all that He promised. There has not failed one word of all His good promise, which He promised through His servant Moses.

- Psalm 89:34

    - My covenant I will not break,
      Nor alter the word that has gone out of
      My lips.

- Psalm 91:10–11; 15–16 (read the whole psalm)

    - No evil shall befall you,
      Nor shall any plague come near your dwelling;
      For He shall give His angels charge over you,
      To keep you in all your ways.
      He shall call upon Me, and I will answer him;
      I will be with him in trouble;
      I will deliver him and honor him.
      With long life I will satisfy him,
      And show him My salvation.

- Psalm 105:37

    - He also brought them out with silver and gold,
      And there was none feeble among His tribes.

- Psalm 107:20

    - He sent His word and healed them,
      And delivered them from their destructions.

- Psalm 118:17

    - I shall not die, but live,
      And declare the works of the Lord.

- Proverbs 3:5

    - Trust in the Lord with all your heart,
      And lean not on your own understanding.

- Proverbs 4:20–22

    - My son, give attention to my words;
      Incline your ear to my sayings.
      Do not let them depart from your eyes;
      Keep them in the midst of your heart;
      For they are life to those who find them,
      And health to all their flesh.

- Isaiah 41:10

    - Fear not, for I am with you;
      Be not dismayed, for I am your God.
      I will strengthen you,
      Yes, I will help you,
      I will uphold you with My righteous
      right hand.

- Isaiah 41:13

    - For I, the Lord your God, will hold your right hand,
      Saying to you, "Fear not, I will help you."

- Isaiah 43:25–26

    - I, even I, am He who blots out your transgressions for My own sake;
      And I will not remember your sins.
      Put Me in remembrance;
      Let us contend together;
      State your case, that you may be acquitted.

- Isaiah 53:5

    - But He was wounded for our transgressions,
      He was bruised for our iniquities;
      The chastisement for our peace was upon Him,

And by His stripes we are healed

- Jeremiah 1:12

    - Then the Lord said to me, "You have seen well, for I am ready to perform My word."

- Jeremiah 30:17

    - "For I will restore health to you
      And heal you of your wounds," says the Lord,
      "Because they called you an outcast saying:
      'This is Zion;
      No one seeks her.'"

- Hosea 4:6

    - My people are destroyed for lack of knowledge.
      Because you have rejected knowledge,
      I also will reject you from being priest for Me;
      Because you have forgotten the law of your God,
      I also will forget your children.

- Joel 3:10

    - Beat your plowshares into swords
      And your pruning hooks into spears;
      Let the weak say, "I am strong."

- Nahum 1:9

    - What do you conspire against the Lord?
      He will make an utter end of it.
      Affliction will not rise up a second time.

- Nahum 1:7

    - The Lord is good,

A stronghold in the day of trouble;
And He knows those who trust in Him.

- Malachi 3:10

  - "Bring all the tithes into the storehouse,
    That there may be food in My house,
    And try Me now in this,"
    Says the Lord of hosts,
    "If I will not open for you the windows of heaven
    And pour out for you such blessing
    That there will not be room enough to receive it."

- Matthew 8:1–3

  - When He had come down from the mountain, great multitudes followed Him. And behold, a leper came and worshiped Him, saying, "Lord, if You are willing, You can make me clean." Then Jesus put out His hand and touched him, saying, "I am willing; be cleansed." Immediately his leprosy was cleansed.

- Matthew 8:17

  - That it might be fulfilled which was spoken by Isaiah the prophet, saying: "He Himself took our infirmities
    And bore our sicknesses."

- Matthew 18:18

  - Assuredly, I say to you, whatever you bind on earth will be bound in heaven, and whatever you loose on earth will be loosed in heaven.

- Matthew 18:19

    - Again I say to you that if two of you agree on earth concerning anything that they ask, it will be done for them by My Father in heaven.

- Matthew 18:20

    - For where two or three are gathered together in My name, I am there in the midst of them.

- Matthew 21:21–22

    - So Jesus answered and said to them, "Assuredly, I say to you, if you have faith and do not doubt, you will not only do what was done to the fig tree, but also if you say to this mountain, 'Be removed and be cast into the sea,' it will be done. And whatever things you ask in prayer, believing, you will receive."

- Mark 11:22–24

    - So Jesus answered and said to them, "Have faith in God. For assuredly, I say to you, whoever says to this mountain, 'Be removed and be cast into the sea,' and does not doubt in his heart, but believes that those things he says will be done, he will have whatever he says. Therefore I say to you, whatever things you ask when you pray, believe that you receive them, and you will have them."

- Mark 16: 17–18

    - "And these signs will follow those who believe: In My name they will cast out demons; they will speak with new tongues; they will take up serpents; and if they drink anything deadly, it will by no means hurt them; they will lay hands on the sick, and they will recover.

- Luke 10:19
    - Behold, I give you the authority to trample on serpents and scorpions, and over all the power of the enemy, and nothing shall by any means hurt you.

- John 10:10
    - The thief does not come except to steal, and to kill, and to destroy. I have come that they may have life, and that they may have it more abundantly.

- John 9:31
    - Now we know that God does not hear sinners; but if anyone is a worshiper of God and does His will, He hears him.

- Romans 4:19–21
    - And not being weak in faith, he did not consider his own body, already dead (since he was about a hundred years old), and the deadness of Sarah's womb. He did not waver at the promise of God through unbelief, but was strengthened in faith, giving glory to God, and being fully convinced that what He had promised He was also able to perform.

- Romans 8:11
    - But if the Spirit of Him who raised Jesus from

the dead dwells in you, He who raised Christ from the dead will also give life to your mortal bodies through His Spirit who dwells in you.

- 2 Corinthians 10:4–5
    - For the weapons of our warfare are not carnal but mighty in God for pulling down strongholds, casting down arguments and every high thing that exalts itself against the knowledge of God, bringing every thought into captivity to the obedience of Christ.
- Galatians 3:13
    - Christ has redeemed us from the curse of the law, having become a curse for us (for it is written, "Cursed is everyone who hangs on a tree").
- Ephesians 6:10–17
    - Finally, my brethren, be strong in the Lord and in the power of His might. Put on the whole armor of God, that you may be able to stand against the wiles of the devil. For we do not wrestle against flesh and blood, but against principalities, against powers, against the rulers of the darkness of this age, against spiritual hosts of wickedness in the heavenly places. Therefore take up the whole armor of God, that you may be able to withstand in the evil day, and having done all, to stand. Stand therefore, having girded your waist with truth, having put on the breastplate of righteousness, and having shod your feet with the preparation of the gospel of peace; above all, taking the shield of faith with

which you will be able to quench all the fiery darts of the wicked one. And take the helmet of salvation, and the sword of the Spirit, which is the word of God.

- Philippians 1:6
  - Being confident of this very thing, that He who has begun a good work in you will complete it until the day of Jesus Christ.
- Philippians 2:13
  - For it is God who works in you both to will and to do for His good pleasure.
- Philippians 4:6–8
  - Be anxious for nothing, but in everything by prayer and supplication, with thanksgiving, let your requests be made known to God; and the peace of God, which surpasses all understanding, will guard your hearts and minds through Christ Jesus. Finally, brethren, whatever things are true, whatever things are noble, whatever things are just, whatever things are pure, whatever things are lovely, whatever things are of good report, if there is any virtue and if there is anything praiseworthy—meditate on these things.
- 2 Timothy 1:7
  - For God has not given us a spirit of fear, but of power and of love and of a sound mind.
- Hebrews 4:12
  - For the word of God is living and powerful,

and sharper than any two-edged sword, piercing even to the division of soul and spirit, and of joints and marrow, and is a discerner of the thoughts and intents of the heart.

- Hebrews 10:23

    - Let us hold fast the confession of our hope without wavering, for He who promised is faithful.

- Hebrews 10:25

    - Not forsaking the assembling of ourselves together, as is the manner of some, but exhorting one another, and so much the more as you see the Day approaching.

- Hebrews 10:35

    - Therefore do not cast away your confidence, which has great reward.

- Hebrews 11:11

    - By faith Sarah herself also received strength to conceive seed, and she bore a child when she was past the age, because she judged Him faithful who had promised.

- Hebrews 13:8

    - Jesus Christ is the same yesterday, today, and forever.

- James 1:5

    - If any of you lacks wisdom, let him ask of God, who gives to all liberally and without reproach, and it will be given to him.

- James 3:17
    - But the wisdom that is from above is first pure, then peaceable, gentle, willing to yield, full of mercy and good fruits, without partiality and without hypocrisy.
- James 4:7–8
    - Therefore submit to God. Resist the devil and he will flee from you. Draw near to God and He will draw near to you. Cleanse your hands, you sinners; and purify your hearts, you double-minded.
- James 5:14
    - Is anyone among you sick? Let him call for the elders of the church, and let them pray over him, anointing him with oil in the name of the Lord.
- 1 Peter 2:9
    - But you are a chosen generation, a royal priesthood, a holy nation, His own special people, that you may proclaim the praises of Him who called you out of darkness into His marvelous light;
- 1 Peter 2:24
    - Who Himself bore our sins in His own body on the tree, that we, having died to sins, might live for righteousness—by whose stripes you were healed.
- 1 Peter 5:7–9
    - Casting all your care upon Him, for He cares

and sharper than any two-edged sword, piercing even to the division of soul and spirit, and of joints and marrow, and is a discerner of the thoughts and intents of the heart.

- Hebrews 10:23

    - Let us hold fast the confession of our hope without wavering, for He who promised is faithful.

- Hebrews 10:25

    - Not forsaking the assembling of ourselves together, as is the manner of some, but exhorting one another, and so much the more as you see the Day approaching.

- Hebrews 10:35

    - Therefore do not cast away your confidence, which has great reward.

- Hebrews 11:11

    - By faith Sarah herself also received strength to conceive seed, and she bore a child when she was past the age, because she judged Him faithful who had promised.

- Hebrews 13:8

    - Jesus Christ is the same yesterday, today, and forever.

- James 1:5

    - If any of you lacks wisdom, let him ask of God, who gives to all liberally and without reproach, and it will be given to him.

- James 3:17
    - But the wisdom that is from above is first pure, then peaceable, gentle, willing to yield, full of mercy and good fruits, without partiality and without hypocrisy.
- James 4:7–8
    - Therefore submit to God. Resist the devil and he will flee from you. Draw near to God and He will draw near to you. Cleanse your hands, you sinners; and purify your hearts, you double-minded.
- James 5:14
    - Is anyone among you sick? Let him call for the elders of the church, and let them pray over him, anointing him with oil in the name of the Lord.
- 1 Peter 2:9
    - But you are a chosen generation, a royal priesthood, a holy nation, His own special people, that you may proclaim the praises of Him who called you out of darkness into His marvelous light;
- 1 Peter 2:24
    - Who Himself bore our sins in His own body on the tree, that we, having died to sins, might live for righteousness—by whose stripes you were healed.
- 1 Peter 5:7–9
    - Casting all your care upon Him, for He cares

for you. Be sober, be vigilant; because your adversary the devil walks about like a roaring lion, seeking whom he may devour. Resist him, steadfast in the faith, knowing that the same sufferings are experienced by your brotherhood in the world.

- 1 John 3:21–22

    - Beloved, if our heart does not condemn us, we have confidence toward God. And whatever we ask we receive from Him, because we keep His commandments and do those things that are pleasing in His sight.

- 1 John 5:14–15

    - Now this is the confidence that we have in Him, that if we ask anything according to His will, He hears us. And if we know that He hears us, whatever we ask, we know that we have the petitions that we have asked of Him.

- 3 John 1:2

    - Beloved, I pray that you may prosper in all things and be in health, just as your soul prospers.

- Revelation 12:11

    - And they overcame him by the blood of the Lamb and by the word of their testimony, and they did not love their lives to the death.

- Matthew 9:20–22

    - And suddenly, a woman who had a flow of blood for twelve years came from behind and touched the hem of His garment. For she said to herself, "If only I may touch His garment, I shall be made well." But Jesus turned around, and when He saw her He said, "Be of good cheer, daughter; your faith has made you well." And the woman was made well from that hour.

- Matthew 8:5–13

    • Now when Jesus had entered Capernaum, a centurion came to Him, pleading with Him, saying, "Lord, my servant is lying at home paralyzed, dreadfully tormented." And Jesus said to him, "I will come and heal him."
    The centurion answered and said, "Lord, I am not worthy that You should come under my roof. But only speak a word, and my servant will be healed. For I also am a man under authority, having soldiers under me. And I say to this one, 'Go,' and he goes; and to another, 'Come,' and he comes; and to my servant, 'Do this,' and he does it."
    When Jesus heard it, He marveled, and said to those who followed, "Assuredly, I say to you, I have not found such great faith, not even in Israel! And I say to you that many will come from east and west, and sit down with Abraham, Isaac, and Jacob in the kingdom of heaven. But the sons of the kingdom will be cast out into outer darkness. There will be weeping and gnashing of teeth." Then Jesus said to the centurion, "Go your way; and as you have believed, so let it be done for you." And his servant was healed that same hour.

- 2 Kings 20:5
    - Return and tell Hezekiah the leader of My people, "Thus says the Lord, the God of David your father: 'I have heard your prayer, I have seen your tears; surely I will heal you. On the third day you shall go up to the house of the Lord.'"
- Psalm 18:2
    - The Lord is my rock and my fortress and my deliverer;
    My God, my strength, in whom I will trust;
    My shield and the horn of my salvation,
    my stronghold.
- Psalm 30:2
    - O Lord my God, I cried out to You,
    And You healed me.
- Psalm 103:1–5
    - Bless the Lord, O my soul;
    And all that is within me, bless His holy name!
    Bless the Lord, O my soul,
    And forget not all His benefits:
    Who forgives all your iniquities,
    Who heals all your diseases,
    Who redeems your life from destruction,
    Who crowns you with lovingkindness and tender mercies,
    Who satisfies your mouth with good things,
    So that your youth is renewed like the eagle's.

- Psalm 107:18–20

    - Their soul abhorred all manner of food,
      And they drew near to the gates of death.
      Then they cried out to the Lord in their trouble,
      And He saved them out of their distresses.
      He sent His word and healed them,
      And delivered them from their destructions.

- Psalm 121:1–2

    - I will lift up my eyes to the hills from whence comes my help?
      My help comes from the Lord,
      Who made heaven and earth.

- Psalm 147:3

    - He heals the brokenhearted
      And binds up their wounds.

- Isaiah 40:31

    - But those who wait on the Lord
      Shall renew their strength;
      They shall mount up with wings like eagles,
      They shall run and not be weary,
      They shall walk and not faint.

- Psalm 138:8

    - The Lord will perfect that which concerns me;
      Your mercy, O Lord, endures forever;
      Do not forsake the works of Your hands.

ENDNOTES

1. Oxford English Dictionary, 'Attend.' Oxford English Dictionary. Oxford University Press, 2024.

2. Oxford English Dictionary, "Incline." Oxford English Dictionary. Oxford University Press, 2024.

3. April Osteen Simons. 2022. "Healing Scriptures with Dodie Osteen EXTENDED VERSION | April Osteen Simons | 2024." YouTube. June 4, 2022. https://www.youtube.com/watch?v=sRF2BseVq6k.

4. Oxford English Dictionary, "Fervently." Oxford English Dictionary. Oxford University Press, 2024.

5. Oxford English Dictionary, "Enthusiasm." Oxford English Dictionary. Oxford University Press, 2024.

ABOUT THE AUTHOR

Janeé Williams is a DMV native and holds a Bachelor's in English Arts from Hampton University and a Master's in Literature, Language, and the Humanities from Marymount University. She is the third child of Baltimore, Maryland, natives Ronald and Crystal Williams and has two older siblings and one younger sibling. She currently works as an Associate Director for a D.C. non-profit and is actively involved in her church. In June of 2023, Janeé was diagnosed with stage 3 breast cancer. She made a choice to stand on God's Word and trust that He would carry her through. This is her first book, and she is blessed to reveal the revelations, plans, and abundant love of the Father that she experienced as she walked through this joyous trial.

www.ingramcontent.com/pod-product-compliance
Lightning Source LLC
LaVergne TN
LVHW010931300125
802500LV00006B/143